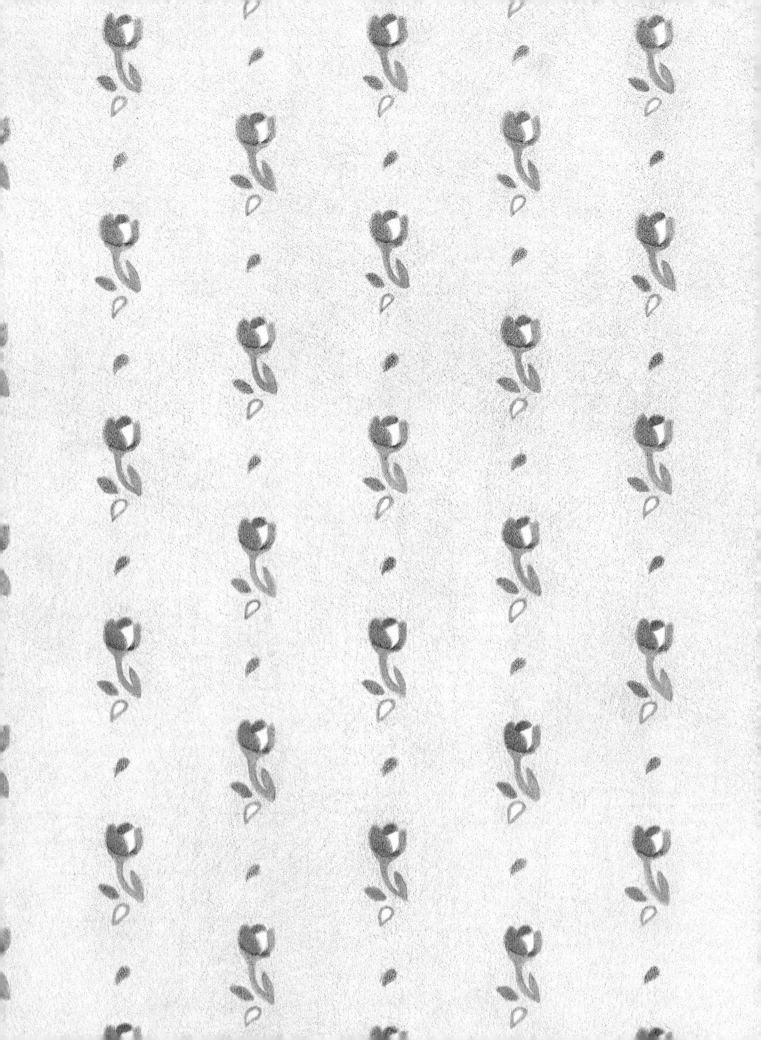

JOSEPH AND ANNA'S
TIME CAPSULE
A Legacy from Old Jewish Prague

Chaya M. Burstein

Illustrated by
Nancy Edwards Calder

Edited by
Linda A. Altshuler and Marjorie L. Share

SUMMIT BOOKS
New York

SMITHSONIAN INSTITUTION
TRAVELING EXHIBITION SERVICE
Washington

This book was published in conjunction with a major exhibition, The Precious Legacy: Judaic Treasures from the Czechoslovak State Collections, *organized by the Smithsonian Institution Traveling Exhibition Service, Anna R. Cohn, project director, in cooperation with Project Judaica, Mark E. Talisman, chairman, and the Ministry of Culture of the Czech Socialist Republic, the Federal Ministry of Foreign Affairs of the Czechoslovak Socialist Republic, the National Committee of the Capital of Prague, and the State Jewish Museum in Prague. Philip Morris Incorporated is the national corporate sponsor of the exhibition.*

Published by SUMMIT BOOKS, a division of Simon & Schuster, Inc.
Simon & Schuster Building
1230 Avenue of the Americas
New York, NY 10020

Summit Books and colophon are trademarks of Simon & Schuster, Inc. Manufactured in the United States of America.

10 9 8 7 6 5 4 3 2 1

Library of Congress Cataloging in Publication Data

Burstein, Chaya M.
  Joseph and Anna's time capsule.

  Published in conjunction with The Precious Legacy—Judaic Treasures from the Czechoslovak State Collections, an exhibition organized by the Smithsonian Institution Traveling Exhibition Service.

  Summary: Two children describe their life in a Jewish community in Prague in 1845, as Judaic objects from Czechoslovak State Collections are depicted. Readers are encouraged to make a time capsule of similar objects of their time for future generations.

  1. Jews—Czechoslovakia—Prague—Social life and customs—Juvenile literature. 2. Judaism—Czechoslovakia—Prague—Customs and practices—Juvenile literature. 3. Prague (Czechoslovakia)—Social life and customs—Juvenile literature. [1. Jews—Czechoslovakia—Prague—Social life and customs. 2. Prague (Czechoslovakia)—Social life and customs] I. Calder, Nancy Edwards, ill. II. Altshuler, Linda A. III. Share, Marjorie L., 1950–   . IV. Smithsonian Institution. Traveling Exhibition Service. V. Title.
  DS135.C96P713   1984   305.8'924'0437
  84-126
  ISBN 0-671-50712-5

Contents

Introduction: Time Capsule

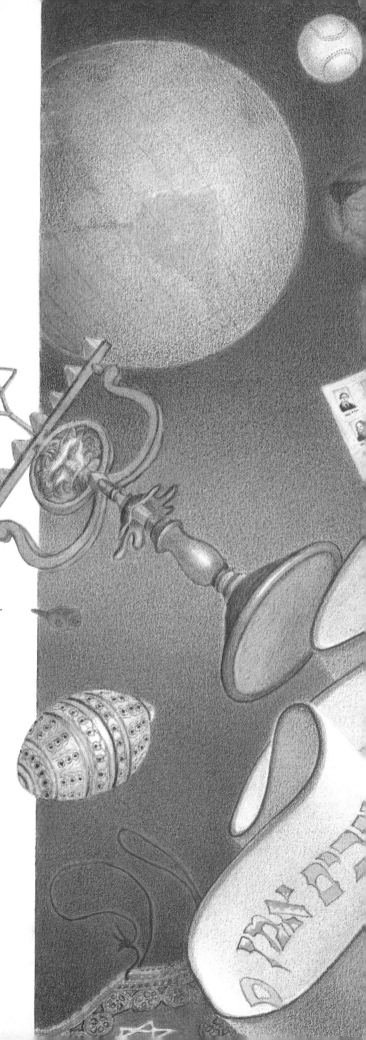

This book is like a time capsule, filled with pictures and descriptions of objects from a faraway time and place. The objects were all used during the eighteenth and nineteenth centuries in the beautiful European city of Prague, in present day Czechoslovakia.

Don't be afraid to read on. Time capsules aren't dangerous. They are simply containers packed full of information and objects that tell about a particular time and place. They may be buried in the ground for people to find in the far future, or stored in the attic to be opened in years to come.

Some capsules are even shot into space. In 1977 American scientists launched the *Voyager* spacecraft. A hundred million light years from today the *Voyager* may come to rest on a planet in a distant galaxy. Intelligent beings will climb all over it, sniffing, poking, and exploring. One of them may find the time capsule that scientists placed in the hull. It is a recording of earth sounds that will fill the air with the natural sounds of roaring lions, crowing roosters, and great, thundering waterfalls, and the man-made sounds of rock-and-roll, folk, and symphonic music. Jimmy Carter—who was our president when the time capsule was launched—will greet listeners in the name of all earthlings. Another voice will tell them about our planet, its history, people, and culture.

4

We do not know how these space beings will react. Perhaps they will be curious, surprised, or amused. But our recorded message will have served the purpose of every time capsule—to explain our lives and our world to someone unfamiliar with them.

Many time capsules are buried right here on earth. Officials at the 1939 New York World's Fair buried a capsule that will be opened in 6939—almost 5,000 years from now. It contains everyday things like comic books and footballs, as well as things of scientific and cultural interest. If New Yorkers have forgotten how to play football in 5,000 years, this capsule will tell them about today's teams and how they play the game. Who knows—the time capsule could start a great intergalactic football league!

Let's imagine that Joseph, who is twelve years old, and Anna, who is ten, are two lively, creative children who lived in Prague in 1845. If Joseph and Anna had known about time capsules, they might have packed a box with books, clothing, dishes, and other objects that told about their lives, then buried the box under the cobblestones in the courtyard of their house. You and I might have dug it up, examined the contents, and tried to understand Joseph and Anna's lives and culture.

That's a lot of imagining. As far as we know, the children of Prague didn't bury time capsules. Instead, the objects in this book were collected from homes and synagogues in and around the city of Prague. They are cared for and displayed in the State Jewish Museum there. From that collection we have selected objects that bring to life Joseph and Anna's legacy from old Jewish Prague.

Some of the objects that you'll find on these pages may seem strange. Some will be familiar, like the things you use in your home, school, synagogue, church, or neighborhood. When you read the stories that Joseph tells about himself, his adventures with his sister Anna, and life in his community, you'll understand how and why each thing was used. At the end of the book try to match each object from Prague with modern objects that you might want to put into your time capsule. Maybe you'll find that you have a lot in common with Joseph and Anna of old Prague.

Prague and its Jewish Quarter

This is me, Joseph, sitting on the high-backed chair and holding a prayer book. I'm nearly thirteen. My sister Anna, who is ten, is sitting on the stool. We're dressed up in our holiday clothing because we are having our portraits painted. Mama keeps saying, "Sit up straight and think about serious things. No giggling!" It's hard for us to sit still for so long.

As soon as the painter packs up his easel, Anna and I change into our everyday clothes and run downstairs to play. Our house is in the middle of the Jewish Quarter of Prague, right near the Town Hall. My sister, my mother and father, my father's helper, and I all live on the third floor. More families live above us. The poorer they are, the higher up they live. That means they have plenty of stairs to climb because our houses are so tall that the roofs seem to lean over and bump into each other. We are crowded because for many years Jews have been allowed to live only in the Jewish Quarter, so the houses have been built tall and close together.

There is one good thing about being close together. It's a short walk to school and friends' homes. The public bath and ritual bath are also around the corner. And the Altneu Synagogue, the Town Hall, and the marketplace are close by, too. Even our cemetery is crowded. Mama says there are twelve layers of people buried in the graves, one above the other. But they surely don't mind. They're in the only sunny, grassy spot in the neighborhood.

The city of Prague spreads out all around our quarter and across the river. When Mama sends us down to buy potatoes or get a bucket of water, Anna and I stop to watch the wagons and carts come across the bridge. They may be loaded with satin cloth or furs or precious metals for our tailors and goldsmiths. The wagons and carts come from the ends of the Austro-Hungarian Empire, maybe further.

Everything comes to Prague because it's such a big city. There are busy marketplaces, tall churches and government buildings, and the palaces of counts and princes and rich merchants. The great and beautiful Prague Castle, where kings and emperors once lived, sits on a hill above the city. Papa says it has a wide courtyard filled with splashing fountains, and statues of horses and kings and queens. Someday, when we are a little older, Anna and I will climb up and look at the castle and explore the rest of Prague, too.

Home

Here is how to find our house. Look for the door with the sign shaped like scissors hanging over it. That's Mendl the tailor's sign. He lives on the fifth floor. Underneath it you'll see another sign with a yellow scale—that's Papa's. He is a goldsmith. In the workroom behind the kitchen he and his helper tap with tiny hammers and shape the metal all day long. But before the Sabbath and the other holidays they stop work early in the afternoon and hurry to the bathhouse and then go to the synagogue.

Anna and I love holidays. All our cousins and aunts and uncles come to visit, and Mama prepares special foods. There is no school, so we can be with our family and listen to Grandpa's stories and take walks with our friends. Passover, the celebration of freedom, is my favorite holiday. It comes in the spring when we are free from the cold winter, and it reminds us that we were once slaves but now we're free.

Mama and Papa start preparing weeks ahead. Papa fills jugs with cherries to make special Passover wine. Mama opens the shutters wide to let in the spring breeze. She empties the cabinets and scrubs the furniture and walls. Anna and I unpack the special dishes and pots that are used only during Passover. My favorite is the blue-and-white seder plate that sits in the center of the table holding Passover foods.

At last it's Passover eve. A white cloth covers the table and on it there are silver candlesticks, a plate of hard, flat Passover bread called matzah, a goblet of Papa's good wine, and the gleaming seder plate. The whole family sits around the table. We have a guest, too. It is a tradition to invite people to share the holiday meal. He is wearing a turban and a striped robe, and came all the way from the Land of Israel.

Mama lights the holiday candles and Papa says the blessing over the wine. Then we read in our Passover books about how our ancestors were freed from slavery in Egypt. We sing happy songs, drink wine, and eat Mama's chicken soup with dumplings, peppery potato pudding, and fish patties. Then the guest tells us about the holy city of Jerusalem where one wall of King Solomon's Temple is still standing. He has touched this famous wall and prayed beside it.

"May we be in Jerusalem next year!" we all call out at the end of the Passover meal.

Baby Wrapper to Torah Binder

It's nice to relax during holidays because we study so hard at school all the rest of the time. Continuing my studies is one of the three important wishes my parents have for me during my life, along with getting married someday, and doing good deeds.

Mama embroidered these wishes on a long band of cloth. She made the band from the sheet in which I was wrapped after I was born. Then she embroidered my name, Papa's name, the date I was born, and my zodiac sign onto the band. When I was much smaller I brought the wrapper as a gift to the Altneu Synagogue, where my family and many people in the community pray. Next year, when I'm thirteen, the community will welcome me as an adult member. I'll read from the Torah scroll, which contains the first five books of the Hebrew Bible. We will wrap the Torah with my embroidered band in honor of my special day.

The first wish on the band, "study," means that I will go to school each day and learn to read and write in Hebrew. That's the ancient language of our holy books. I study these books to learn about our history and religion, and how to follow all of our customs so that I can live a good Jewish life. "Marriage" is the second wish. I'm not thinking too much about that yet. "Good deeds" is the third wish. I really try to be helpful. I even help Anna. But she doesn't remember when I'm nice—just when I'm not.

School

Anna and I both go to a school that is run by our Jewish community. We are in different grades, and since boys and girls are in separate classes, I do not see her much. We study all sorts of subjects: history, geography, mathematics, and science. But we must not forget our Jewish studies. I am preparing to read from the Torah scroll next year so I must learn Hebrew, Bible, and Jewish history. That's a lot of extra subjects, but my friends Jacob and Simon work with me.

Our teacher tells us that Prague has been an important center of Jewish learning for hundreds of years, and we must help to carry on the tradition. Prague had the first Hebrew printing press in Central Europe and made beautiful books that were sent all over the world. Some very old books are still in Prague, but they are too fragile for us to use in our classes.

When my friends and I turn thirteen and are called up to read the Torah in the synagogue we won't read from an ordinary book. We will read from a long scroll which is wound around two carved posts. The scroll is made of thin leather called parchment. It is not printed on a printing press, but written by hand with a quill pen.

Our teacher says these scrolls are very precious and take many months to copy. We honor them as though they are kings and queens. When we finish reading the scrolls we roll them up tightly, tie them with the binder, and cover them with a velvet mantle sparkling with gold embroidery and jewels. Then we place a breastplate and a crown with tinkling bells on each scroll, and put them into their closet on the eastern wall of the synagogue.

Mama and Papa are proud of my work at school and want me to go on to the university. They want me to be well educated.

15

The Altneu Synagogue

Our synagogue is 600 years old—the oldest one in the Jewish Quarter. People tell many spooky stories about it. Mama's helper Sarah says that there has never been a fire in the synagogue even though there are often fires in the Jewish Quarter. She says two white doves guard the roof. When fire breaks out nearby they coo loudly to warn the people.

Lazer the apprentice told me that a secret thing is hidden in the synagogue attic. Nobody is allowed to go up to see it. It has been there for nearly 300 years, since the time of Rabbi Judah Loew. In those years the Jewish Quarter was often attacked by enemies. Rabbi Loew prayed for help, and God told him to make a powerful, gigantic creature, a golem, out of the clay of the riverbank. The golem lumbered through the streets of the Jewish Quarter and drove the enemies out. He dragged other troublemakers off to jail. The golem's work was done. But he couldn't stop. He grew wild and started to smash buildings and frighten people.

Rabbi Loew sadly commanded the golem to climb up to the attic of the Altneu Synagogue. With a magic word he turned the giant back into a heap of clay. Then he covered the clay with old holy books and prayer shawls. When he came down from the attic he gave a firm command, "Nobody may ever go up to the attic again!"

I go to the Altneu Synagogue with Papa some weekday mornings and every Sabbath morning. Men stand on the cobblestone street in front talking about ships and cargo, the price of gold, and the news from Amsterdam or Vienna. My friends Jacob and Simon play tag in the crowd. Papa and I brush past them and step down into the cool, dim hall of the synagogue. There are few windows, so the light comes from hanging candelabra. The synagogue is taller and grander from the inside because the floor is sunken below the street level, since the government authorities do not allow us to build synagogues as tall as churches.

Ahead of us in the middle of the room the prayer-leader stands on a raised platform reading from the prayer book. A red banner hangs over his head. It has a six-pointed star with a Swedish cap embroidered in the center. We're very proud of that banner. In 1648 Emperor Ferdinand III gave our people the right to display it for helping him drive off his Swedish enemies.

People are swaying back and forth as they pray at the reading tables around the platform. Papa and I begin to pray too, but I can't pay attention to the words. Instead I find myself looking up at the prayer-leader. In a few months I'll be standing beside him reading from the Torah scroll, in the same spot where Rabbi Loew stood when he prayed for God's help many years ago.

Good Deeds

As my father and I leave the synagogue after the service we pass the charity box. Its long arm seems to reach right into our pockets. Papa murmurs a saying of our wise men, "If I am not for myself, who will be for me? But if I am only for myself then what good am I?" On weekdays he drops in coins, but on the Sabbath we may not carry money.

Mama also remembers charity and good deeds. Every few days she sends me or Anna up to Mendl the tailor's apartment to bring his family some potatoes or a herring. Mendl is too sick to work, and his wife Bayleh earns only a few coins each day selling old clothes in the marketplace. Just last Sabbath afternoon Bayleh and Mama were sitting together. Bayleh was wiping her eyes and looked very sad. I heard her say, "How will my daughter be able to marry when I have no money to pay for a wedding?" Mama patted her shoulder. "Don't worry," she said, "the people of our community will provide money for your daughter's marriage."

That's how it is in the Jewish Quarter. We like to do things to help each other. We have a special society that helps to pay for weddings for poor and orphaned girls. And there's a society to visit and comfort the sick. Another society helps to prepare the dead for burial. Even on holidays and other happy occasions we share our joy by putting money in the charity box.

The richer a person is, the more he is supposed to help. Once, a very rich, important man named Mordecai Maisel lived in our community. He built the bathhouse, the ritual bath, a house for poor people, and several synagogues. Then he paved all the streets with stone.

If I ever get rich I'll do a lot of good deeds, too. And even if I'm never rich I'll do good deeds. Who knows, I may need help from others someday. I won't forget because the Torah wrapper will always remind me of ". . . study, marriage, and good deeds."

Clocks and
Two Worlds

When Anna and I were little, before we visited parts of Prague outside our neighborhood, we thought that our town hall was the biggest, most beautiful building in the whole world. It has gables and columns and a tile roof, and it's topped by a steeple with a bell. A six-pointed Star of David on the steeple's peak towers over the whole Jewish Quarter.

Our town hall even has two clocks. The large one on the steeple has Roman numerals and hands that move in the usual way. But the clock on the roof is special. It has Hebrew letters instead of numbers, and its hands move in exactly the opposite direction of most clock hands. That's because Hebrew is written from right to left, exactly the opposite of German and Czech.

Anna and I like to go with Papa when he sells jewelry in the big marketplace. We dodge between shiny carriages and rough farm wagons to get there. It is always crowded with shoppers and stands of fruits, vegetables, cloth, ribbons, and flowers.

Women sell sausages and beer and talk in Czech. Papa can speak a few words of Czech, but Anna and I know only the two languages we speak in the Jewish Quarter: German and our special German-Jewish language. We keep Hebrew for study and prayer. One day I was brave and used sign language to buy two yellow ribbons for Anna. Then, while Papa worked, we sat close beside him and stared at the great, gray buildings and the busy square.

Churches with tall spires surround the marketplace. Many towers reach into the sky from the rooftops—bell towers, clock towers, church towers—a forest of towers. The buildings are big and somber with thick columns and great, heavy arches. But funny little stone heads grin from the corners. They make us laugh.

The Prague Town Hall is much bigger than the one in the Jewish Quarter, and it has an even stranger clock. The face is painted with the signs of the zodiac. When it strikes the hour, two little windows open, and tiny figures come out to parade in a circle, and then a rooster pops out of a window at the top of the clock and crows.

We return to the Jewish Quarter as the evening bells ring from the castle on the hill. "Shalom, welcome," people call, and wave to us. "Shalom to you," we call back. It's good to be home, but when we look up at the Altneu Synagogue and our town hall with its Hebrew clock and modest steeple they no longer seem large. We once told Papa that our neighborhood seemed small and unimportant.

"Tiny it is," he said, smiling, "but to us it's very important. It makes us doubly blessed. We have two worlds— the world of Jewish culture and the larger world of the great city of Prague."

You And Your World

Now that you have met Joseph and Anna and have become familiar with their lives, you can learn more by looking at the objects from Prague. Joseph and Anna have left their time capsule for you. It is their precious legacy.

As you read about the objects in this section, you may discover that you have similar things in your life that can tell others about your world today. You, too, have a precious legacy worth preserving for the future.

In fact, you can bury a capsule of your own, either for future generations or for a future you. Choose a few objects that will tell the most about you, using the activities in this book as a guide. Label your objects so that you and others will be able to identify them years from now. Write on a piece of cardboard the object's name, maker, date, and any other clues to what it is and what it means.

What kind of container will you use for your time capsule? Some possibilities include a heavy cardboard box, large plastic container with lid, small suitcase, metal storage box, or file cabinet.

Just as the objects from nineteenth-century Prague were kept in museums and storerooms, your things must be stored carefully. You don't want them to get ruined over the years. Depending on the kind of container you use, you can bury your capsule in the ground, put it in an attic, hide it in a trunk, or simply place it on a shelf for safekeeping.

Drawing of old Jewish Prague.

Putting Yourself on the Map

The Jewish Quarter of Prague is so small that Joseph and Anna knew every corner. They could easily walk to all the places that were important to them.

Look carefully at the maps of Prague. They may seem a little strange at first, since the language and places are unfamiliar. Some maps are fancy and others are plain. Do the buildings and winding streets tell you anything about the city?

Plan to make a map of your own neighborhood. List all the places that you see or visit every week, including school, home, friends' houses, markets, play areas, religious center, favorite shops, and places where your parents work.

Now, using a sheet of graph paper, ruler, and pencil, try to draw buildings, parks, streets, and other familiar sites in your area. Could a stranger use your map to find important places in your neighborhood?

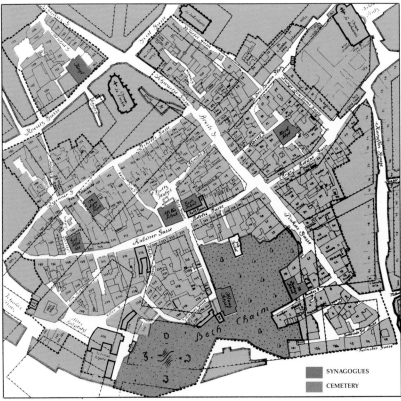

SYNAGOGUES
CEMETERY

This street map of the Jewish Quarter in the 1800s shows the cemetery, eight synagogues, and other important community buildings.

Pictures Worth A Thousand Words

Cameras were still a new invention when Joseph and Anna were children in Prague. Therefore, to capture someone's likeness and personality, artists usually painted portraits. In nine-teenth-century portraits, peo-ple—like the two children pictured—appeared stiff and somber. They wanted people who saw the portraits to take them seriously.

Today, photographic por-traits are usually less expen-sive and more popular than painted portraits. We are also accustomed to informal snap-shots. Portraits, whether painted or photographed, record a person's character, physical appearance, and sometimes his or her occupa-

The children in these nineteenth-century portrait paintings are staring out at us solemnly. Their hair is neatly combed and they are dressed up.

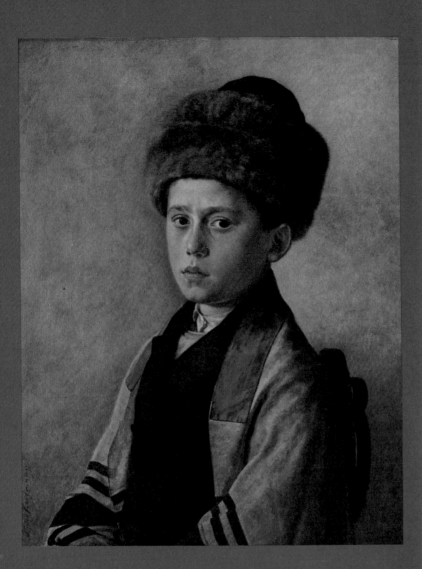

Family portrait, photographed about 1900.

tion or hobby. People sitting for formal portraits even hold props to suggest what is important to them.

Ask a friend or family member to take pictures of you with black-and-white or color film to include in your time capsule. Look at the pictures around your house to get ideas. Carefully choose clothing, background, setting, facial expression, props, and whether you want to look formal or casual. These are some of the clues that the person finding your photograph in the time capsule will use to find out about you.

After your film is developed, carefully label the photographs and store them with your other objects.

Let's Celebrate

Cousins, grandparents, and other family members and friends gathered at Joseph and Anna's house for the holidays. At the Passover seder they celebrated freedom, sang, and ate together. Special foods were prepared. At such festivals, customs and traditions are passed from one generation to the next.

The best-known holidays are religious, ethnic, and national. You probably have several that you share with your friends and family. On the Fourth of July, for example, we remember the colonists' struggle for freedom, and celebrate it with barbecues, bonfires, and noisy fireworks. At Thanksgiving we feast on turkey, cranberries, sweet potatoes, and other good food in honor of the Pilgrims and the fall harvest.

You may also have special traditions—stories, keepsakes, activities, photographs, ways of saying things—that no one outside your family knows about. Does your family celebrate birthdays, graduations, births, or good news in special ways?

What objects could you gather for your time capsule to tell a story about your family's traditional way of celebrating? Find two objects and put them away with a label.

During Joseph and Anna's Passover meal, there was a guest who brought them news of faraway places. Many years ago news was carried from town to town by travelers. This took a long time. News could be outdated before it reached its destination. How do you get your news today? You learn a lot from family, friends, and teachers, but you also have many impersonal sources. These include television, radio, satellites, computers, newspapers, and magazines. Which do you use the most? Put a description of your favorite source and a story from this source in your time capsule. Imagine the excitement when you or someone twenty-five years from now discovers your story.

This Passover seder plate, made in the late 1800s, held foods that told the story of this springtime holiday of freedom.

From Baby
to Binder

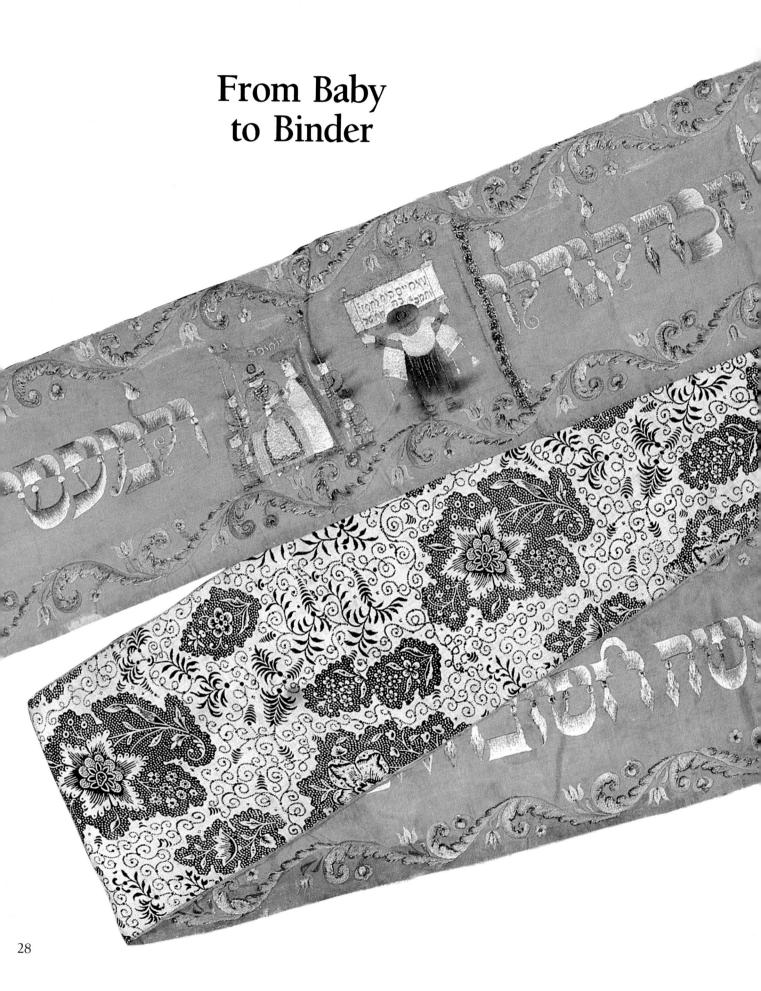

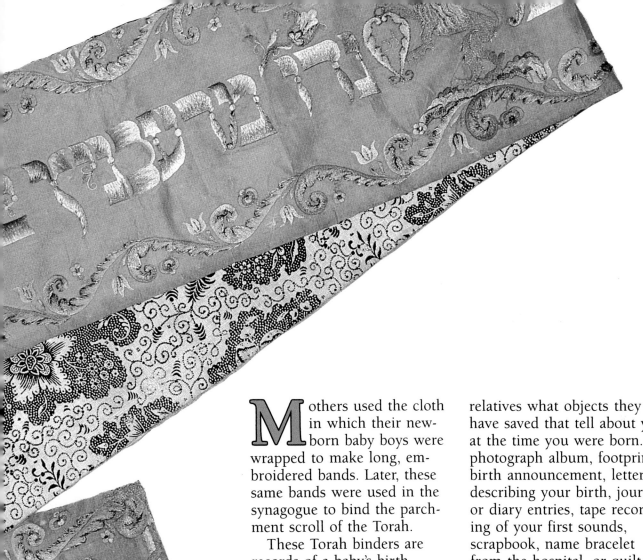

others used the cloth in which their newborn baby boys were wrapped to make long, embroidered bands. Later, these same bands were used in the synagogue to bind the parchment scroll of the Torah.

These Torah binders are records of a baby's birth. Today a birth certificate provides this information. The paper, however, does not carry parents' wishes for the child's future as Joseph's binder did. Ask your parents and relatives what objects they have saved that tell about you at the time you were born. A photograph album, footprint, birth announcement, letter describing your birth, journal or diary entries, tape recording of your first sounds, scrapbook, name bracelet from the hospital, or quilt with an inscription might give you interesting information. Ask if you may borrow the objects or make copies or photographs of them for your time capsule.

What are your wishes for the future? How do they compare with your parents' dreams for you? Are they different from what Joseph and Anna's parents wished—study, marriage, and good deeds?

A loving aunt made this Torah binder in 1749/50 for her nephew Samuel.

*Glass stones and sequins, velvet and silk ribbon, and metal bells
decorate this silk Torah curtain made in 1824/5.*

Special Interests

The Torah scroll is the oldest and most beloved of all Jewish sacred writings. It is kept in the synagogue in a special closet called an ark. Three times each week the scroll is taken out and read. Craftsmen make beautiful curtains, mantles, shields, and crowns in which to dress Torah scrolls. Readers use silver pointers to follow the words so as not to soil the parchment with their fingers.

Studying the Bible and learning to read from the Torah scrolls were important to Joseph and his friends. They planned to continue studying them even after their formal religious training ended. You may have a special interest that you will continue to learn about as you grow older. Select an object that represents your interest and put it inside your time capsule.

A decorated page from the Prague Pentateuch, printed in 1530 by the Gersonides family, who founded in Prague the first Hebrew press north of the Alps.

Joseph and Anna studied in school from early morning until sundown. They shared books with other students and memorized many of their lessons. Some parts of going to school are the same today as they were a century ago. Do you think that there are some activities like memorizing and taking tests that students do no matter where or when they live?

But many things about going to school have changed. Do you have televisions, tapes, and other equipment in your school that would seem mysterious to Joseph and Anna? Choose and label one or two objects—or pictures of objects—that you think are different from what Joseph and Anna had, that will tell someone who finds your time capsule something about your life at school.

Signs, Symbols, and Superheroes

For 700 years the Altneu (Old-New) Synagogue has been a place of worship, and a center of community activities in Prague. Meetings and debates as well as religious services are held within its stone walls. The "Swedish" flag is still proudly displayed inside.

Today churches and synagogues are also used for meetings, classes, and concerts. We still use flags and other symbols to give us important information—although we don't always keep them in churches and synagogues. You may have some in your school or home. Choose a flag, emblem, or sticker that represents something—a club, society, school, organization—that is important to you.

The story of the powerful golem is one of the favorite folk tales of Prague. Today, we enjoy stories of superheroes who rescue good people and punish evil ones. Do you have a favorite hero or heroine? Is he or she a make-believe person or a real one? Find photographs, buttons, books, or movie advertisements that tell something about your superheroes for your time capsule. What kind of people do you think children of the future will admire? Who will your heroes be twenty-five years from now? Write down your predictions and include them in the capsule.

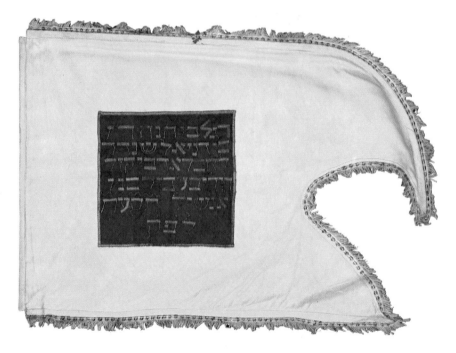

Banner of the Society for Visiting the Sick, made in Bohemia in 1817/8.

In 1648 Emperor Ferdinand III granted the Prague Jewish Community the right to fly this flag, which honors Jewish efforts to defend the city against the invading Swedes. At the flag's center is a six-pointed star surrounding a Swedish cap, an image that has become the coat of arms for the Jews of Prague.

This pewter emblem of the Jewish Butcher's Guild was made in Prague in 1620. Members carried it in public processions and events.

Who could ignore this brass and wood charity box with its outstretched hand? The Hebrew message reads "A gift in secret turns away anger."

מתן בסתר

יכפה אף

Doing
Good Deeds

One of the wishes parents made for their newborn babies in Prague was "to do good deeds." As children grew up they learned to help others by giving money to the poor and to community projects. They also helped by caring for sick people and sheltering travelers.

What are the ways in which you help others? Do you help care for younger or older members of your family? Are you a member of a scout troop? Do you help collect money for local or national charities? Put objects in your time capsule that show how you help others.

Today, people all over the world live without adequate housing, medical care, or schools. Many do not even have enough to eat.

Do you know of any people who are poor—without family, money, or work? How do they receive help? How do the federal, state, or local governments or private groups help these people?

This wine pitcher was used by the Prague Burial Society for its annual banquets. The members prepared the dead for burial, a task that is considered a great honor.

The two clocks on the Jewish
Town Hall in Prague.

This beautiful synagogue clock was
created in about 1870. The large
central clock keeps time, while the
six smaller dials are set by hand
each week to indicate times of
prayer.

Living
in Different
Worlds

Two different worlds are
represented by the
clocks on the Jewish
Town Hall in Prague. The
clock with Roman numerals
links the Jewish community
to the daily life and business
of the great city of Prague.
But the clock with Hebrew
letters seems to say proudly,
"We have our own Jewish
religious and cultural life here
in the Jewish Quarter, side by
side with the life of the Czech
city around us."

Like Joseph and Anna, you
are part of more than one
world. You are part of a
country, and you are a member of a community, city or
town, school, and family.
Sometimes your own special
group or daily life may seem
like a separate world. And
sometimes you may realize
how many different groups
you are a part of.

Find objects that tie you to
the different worlds around
you to show that you are a
U.S. citizen, or a citizen of
another country, part of a
religious group, part of a town
or city, member of a club,
team, or activity group, and
family member.

Your Time Capsule

After you have shown your objects to an older family member or friend and are happy with what you have, wrap each one with its label for storage. Put them in the container and sign your name on the outside. Now you must locate a special place to keep your capsule. Somewhere in and around your own home may be best, but do not forget the capsule if your family moves.

By learning about how Joseph and Anna lived, you have seen how objects can be a common language, reaching across distance and time. You probably have also found that you have a lot in common with Joseph and Anna—your worlds are not as far apart as you once might have thought. Likewise, your time capsule will help you speak to people in the future, and will pass on your own precious legacy just as Joseph and Anna have shared theirs with you.

Joseph and Anna's Time Capsule was prepared by
the Smithsonian Institution Traveling Exhibition Service
under the direction of Andrea Price Stevens, Publications Officer.

Original illustrations were rendered in watercolor and pencil
by Nancy Calder Edwards.

Designed by Judy Kirpich, Grafik Communications Ltd.,
Alexandria, Virginia.

Studio photographs taken at the State Jewish Museum in Prague by
QuickSilver Photographers, Washington, D.C.:
Mark Gulezian, Alex Jamison, Edward Owen.

Other photographs: p. 25, bottom: State Jewish Museum,
Prague; p. 33, right: Martin Stein, p. 37, Alex Jamison.

Edited by Linda A. Altshuler, director,
B'nai B'rith Klutznick Museum, and Marjorie L. Share,
head, education department, SITES.

Typeset in Berkeley Light by
Carver Photocomposition, Arlington, Virginia.

The assistance of the following colleagues is gratefully acknowledged:
David Altshuler, Mary Beth Byrne, Katherine Chambers, Joan Fram,
Deborah Lerme Goodman, Hillel Kieval, Seymour Rossel, and Claire Wolfman.

Please refer to *The Precious Legacy:
Judaic Treasures from the Czechoslovak State Collections*,
edited by David Altshuler, and published in 1983 by
Summit Books and SITES, for further information.

The catalogue numbers provided here identify the objects in the exhibition and book:
p. 24: cat. 234; p. 25, top: cat. 242; p. 27: cat. 127; p. 28: cat. 34; p. 30: cat. 8; p. 31:
cat. 278; p. 32: cat. 150; p. 33, left: cat. 143; p. 34: cat. 83; p. 35: cat. 161; p. 36: cat. 89.

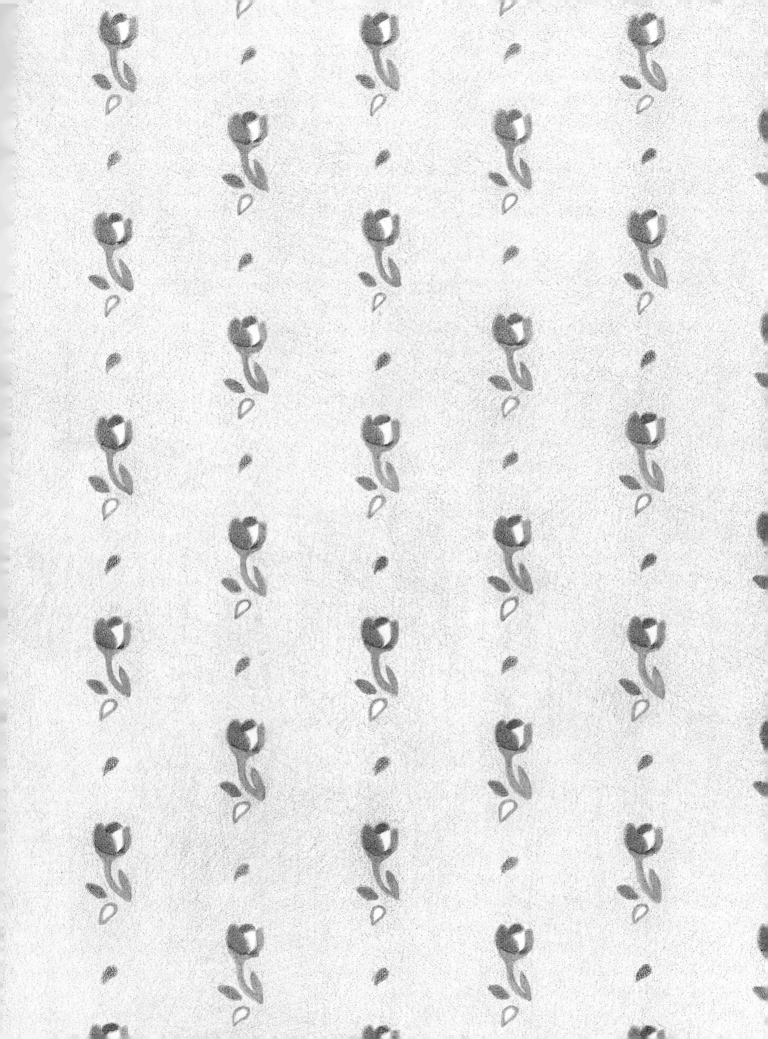

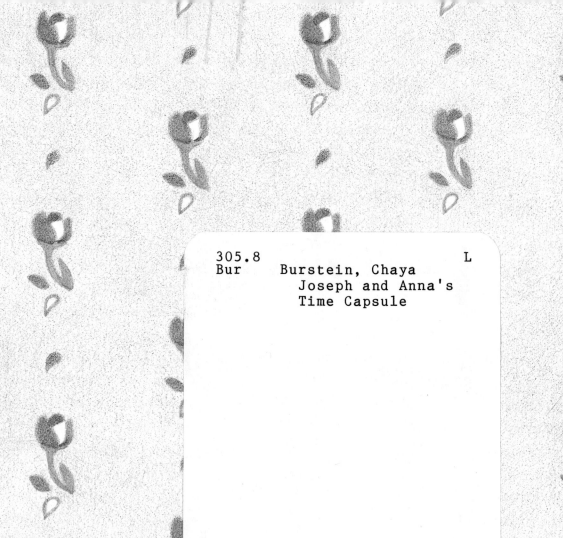